Why Existence?

Peter John Scott

INTRODUCTION

Don't take my word for it, but there is something fishy about this book...

Why Existence?

Peter John Scott

The fishy characters in this book do not exist but in the imagination of the author, and have no relation in any way to anyone bearing the same name or names. Furthermore, they are not inspired by anyone the author has, does know, or is unknown to the author, and all the incidents herein are pure invention.

DEDICATION

Thanks to Michael S Heiser's published work and
to the input numberless other fishes of faith

CONTENTS

1 EXISTENCE

Just where the fish tank is located is not known. Some fish claim that it exists upon the back of a giant turtle, others say that it stands alone in the vastness of somewhere unimaginable. A few fish consider that it floats upon an endless bottomless ocean. No-one seems certain, but it is true to say that most fishes couldn't care less...

Size wise, the fish tank is about two metres long, one metre wide, and including its sloping metal hood, is approximately a metre and a half high.

Peering out of the fish tank from the inside, the glass in the fish tank appears an opaque green.

A bright strip-light revered as 'The Light', sits in the inside of the hood that is positioned above the fish tank, and it illuminates everything under and above the water in a gentle blue glow. Except at night, when it goes out according to a traditional belief that will be explained later. In the morning The Light suddenly shines again, and the darkness vanishes. The Light has always existed, so fish legend has it.

In one corner of the fish tank sits a duel oxygenating pump and a water-filter combined (it was on special offer). It is of a golden hue and is fashioned into the shape of a fairy castle. From its turrets the castle releases a continual thin streams of magical and beautiful bubbles that rush upwards towards the surface, where they pop and disappear. The fishes do not understand how or why this happens, or where the bubbles go to, but it is something to talk about.

In another corner of the fish tank (there being four) is a horizontal heated glass tube that keeps the water pleasantly warm for the thin-blooded occupants as they swim about blupping and blopping.

Many species of fish live in the fish tank, of all differing colours, sizes, natures, and habits.

But before we continue with this fishy tale, there are a few fishy facts that you need to understand - it is not generally appreciated that fish do not recognise each other by the name of their species, these are forms of identification that only we and ichthyologists use.

Fish employ another method of reference altogether - by referring to three notable and distinctive aspects of their appearance. Say, having large scales, beady eyes, and a pointed tail, or a long thin body, black spots, and a blue nose.

So a fishy conversation might go something like this: *"Hey, you there - The fish with the long thin body, black spots, and blue nose. What are you doing today?"*

Then the fish with the long thin body, black spots, and blue nose, might reply, *"Mind your own business, you beady eyed, large scaled, pointed tailed, busy body fish."* And so forth...

However, another added complication to the accurate re-counting of this story, is that, as far as I know, fish do not use human language, but communicate with each other using blups, gesticulations, squeaks, grunts, sonar, or other fishy subaquatic sounds, some even beyond our range of hearing.

But it would be very tedious for me to have to communicate to you what the fish in the fish tank are actually saying to each other. I would be obliged to use a SALTTBTI (scientific aquatic linguistic translation text babble translator). So with your kind permission, and in the interest of a less tedious procedure, I will dispense with the technology and instead, guess.

Despite many of the fish appearing very different from each other the fish in the fish tank exist reasonably well together, apart from a few horrible exceptions, whom we shall meet later.

Reflecting all the colours of the rainbow, or even more, if that was at all possible, some fishes glow vividly, one or two are transparent, a few resemble pink wiggly worms, and others make you laugh.

It is also true to say that to the likes of you and me some of the fish appear to be identical - but from the point of view of a shoaling neon, say, Dad looks nothing like Mum, and Aunty neon does not resemble Grandad, therefore tri-identification family confusion is happily avoided.

Having personalities that vary from placid to 'I will kill you', inherently and sensibly, the fish tend to divide the fish tank into numerous differing areas, or territories, and tend to keep to their own kind, or if not, they prefer their own company.

Divergent types of waterweed grow in the fish tank. Mostly, green, reddish, and brown - Anacharis, Ludwigia, Chiliensis and some other stuff that I can't be bothered to research. Only a small wavy quantity, but enough to make the fish tank appear pleasing, and to give a home to some tiny iridescent red and turquoise neon fish that I have already mentioned and dodge about a lot.

At the bottom of the fish tank lays a thick layer of coloured mixed gravel, composed of intense white, lurid blue, crimson red, and bright green. There is also a quantity of pink sand scattered here and there.

Life in the fish tank is usually uneventful, unless a new fish unexpectedly arrives, or one stops moving for a long time, and is eventually removed by The Net.

The entry of The Net into the depths of the fish tank, is feared by the fish, and considered a bad omen. Subsequently, The Net is to be avoided at all costs.

Should The Net suddenly appear, all the fish accelerate from meander, to a hundred knots in a split second, and in a mad panic dash around in all directions until The Net disappears again.

Once in a morning and once in an evening, a mixture of fish food in the form of appetizing mouth-sized multi-coloured fish-flakes appear upon the surface of the water, and there is an upward dash of hungry residents to eat as much as possible before anybody else does.

Once a week, or so, two thirds of the water in the fish tank is replenished in a mysterious *whooshing* fashion, by a dangerous plunging disturbance that eventually makes the water go from cloudy to clear.

Once this has happened existence goes back to normal for a while until the next *whoosh* arises. Fishes do not know why this happens either.

*

Going about his watery life, an old and solitary cobalt loach is sitting on the gravel at the bottom of the fish tank, ruminating. He is shaded a bluish silver, is of a medium build, and has red eyes – Let's name him Fred, and why not. Compared to the rest of the inhabitants of the fish tank, Fred appears to be nothing out of the ordinary (sorry Fred).

Wandering aimlessly nearby there is a young guppy with a beautiful fan shaped tail that is highlighted with red blotches, he has a silver sheen, and bright yellow eyes - we will name him George.

From time to time through the misty veil of the glass, Fred and George and the other fishes can see fuzzy things moving about outside of the fish tank. To the majority of the inhabitants of the fish tank these objects are of little interest. But to George they are mysterious forms, and have become magical items of speculative thought and conversation.

All in all, Fred fish considers that his aquatic life is normal, mostly peaceful, has always been so, and will continue so to be. Sadly, Fred is deluded.

2 GEORGE

One day down in the depths Fred was quietly minding his own business, eyes out of focus, and intently thinking of nothing. He was methodically selecting one piece of grimy gravel at a time, sucking it clean, before stowing it in a pouch inside his cheek. A slow and satisfying undertaking...

The tranquillity of the morning was interrupted abruptly when out of nowhere George suddenly appeared at Fred's side, "FRED, WHERE DO YOU THINK WE COME FROM?" George asked, loudly. This was a pressing question that had been troubling George for some time.

Now this enquiry was not unreasonable, but the noisy and unwelcome interruption took Fred by surprise and he expelled a mouthful of half processed gravel at great speed, "*BLUP FLUBBING POB*," Fred replied (sorry, there is no respectable translation).

"Sorry?" George said, confused, before continuing as if nothing had happened, "Fred, you seem so old, so you must be very wise, do you know where we fishes come from - every fish seems to have a different theory."

"OLD, ME, OLD?" Fred was not amused, "*Go and ask Bill, George. I'm too busy with important things to consider such trivial matters*," Fred replied, before hovering up another tasty mouthful and turning tail.

George was not keen on the suggestion and pulled a face.

One of the most ancient fish in the fish tank, Bill, was even older than Fred, but unlike Fred, Bill *was* very wise. However, Bill's knowledge was rarely put to the test, for he was not the friendliest of fishes.

Bill had two prominent rows of sharp teeth, he was always in a bad temper, and as far as Bill was concerned, he owned a particular few litres of the fish tank. Consequently, aggressively territorial, it was not unknown for Bill to nip a fin or two before chasing any interloper away.

Amazingly, George's quest outweighed his fear and with serious trepidation he slowly swam to the specific area of the fish tank where he knew Bill would be lurking. It took a while.

After observing Bill from a distance for what seemed an eternity, George bucked up courage and slowly moved towards him.

"Err, err, excuse me, please, Sir," George said, in a loud blupping and rather hesitant voice, still some way off...

Surprised to be disturbed, Bill looked up to see who dared come near, and then lowered his head, bared his teeth a little more, and stared in George's direction.

"Sorry to trouble you... Sir Bill," George, stammered, "...but, will you kindly answer me a question that no fish seems to know a sensible answer to?" George continued, very frightened, "They say that you know everything, and that you are the wisest fish in the fish tank!"

George shut up and prepared to scarper, but fortunately for George, grovelling flattery seemed to be working.

"Well, as you have inquired so politely, and you have not invaded my space, you may ask away, Stranger…" Bill, said, underneath his gaze, "But I wouldn't come too close, if I was you."

"Not likely!" George exclaimed, almost forgetting his place.

"What's that you say?" Bill uttered, moving forwards.

"Nothing, nothing…" George said, swimming backwards until Bill stopped advancing.

Bill pulled an expectant face – "Spit it out, boy," he said.

"OH, Oh, ok - It's just that, you being very wise and all, I thought that you might know why we fish exist, where The Net comes from, and where it takes us when we go motionless?"

Bill frowned, "You said, one question - that's three questions, Sonny," he said, giving himself time to think, not certain of an answer to any of them.

"Oh, and who is The Big Fish, and does He even exist?" George added, expectantly, making the most of his opportunity, and perhaps stretching his luck.

Now, more stumped than ever, Bill was getting confused, and his malevolent snarl morphed into a frustrated expression, "That's five questions, and each one is more stupid than its predecessor," Bill stated pompously, scratching his head with a fin.

"Sorry, Sir," George kind of grinned in embarrassment.

"Look lad, we have all lived before, in another life, in another fish tank - I was a shark, once upon a time, I'll have you know - now shove off."

"Then, who is The Big Fish?" George asked, quickly, and what is the point of life?"

Bill looked thoughtful. He had had little opportunity of conversation over the last few years, and realised that he was enjoying his chat, and relaxed a little, "Well, err, once upon a time we all existed as gravel," Bill announced, quite pleased with his conclusion.

"GRAVEL?" George, was not sure about that one.

Bill grimaced, and added some more doubtful information that had just popped into his imagination, "…and The Big Fish is a starfish!" Bill looked in George's direction to see if George seemed impressed.

"I see, mmm..." George tried to appear convinced - this fish was barmy.

Just then a few flakes of fish food miraculously settled upon the surface of the water, and realising what was happening, in an instant Bill suddenly thrashed his tail, and at great speed, shot up towards the top of the fish tank.

Not really feeling hungry, but anxious not to miss a meal, George followed Bill hood-wards to reach the fishy turmoil, and made a desperate effort to slurp a few bits of floating flake before it all disappeared.

Soon, among a mad scramble of other fish, Bill was nipping fins, and shoving smaller fish out of his way, gulping down his supper for all that he was worth. Bill, worshipped food, to him, it was the only thing that made life liveable.

Swimming around in circles among the melee, George managed to eat a little food, but not as much as he might have liked, and certainly not as much as did the greedy bigger fish.

When supper was over, the fish went their separate ways. Full to the gills, Bill returned to his territory, and remaining hungry, Fred swam back to his gravel sifting.

With a sigh, Fred began searching for any tiny traces of fish food that might have settled to the bottom of the fish tank.

It was time for introspection, but George didn't understand that word, so from a distance, George hung suspended in the centre of the fish tank, contemplating existence.

Beneath, Fred continued to methodically move along the bottom of the fish tank syphoning away. Something Fred had done thousands of times before.

In the watery distance, George could also see Bill, who was harassing a passing slimy loach that minding its own business had accidently drifted into Bills territory.

'This is a hard and an unjust existence,' George philosophised, 'the larger fish bully we smaller fish, and hoover up most of the fish food before we can satisfy our needs. Thus the big fish grow even bigger and torment us all the more – it's not fair!'

George also understood that even though there was plenty of fish food to go around, over time, some weaker fish gave up trying to feed themselves. These tiddlers would grow thinner and thinner, until starved into motionless, The Net would spirit them away somewhere.

Well-fed fish said that starvation was a good thing because that meant that only the strongest fish survived. The phenomenon was referred to as 'spratual selection'. George did not agree with the hypothesis. No, not one bit. But what could be done about it? George needed to find a place to think...

*

"What are you doing loitering about in our waterweed, George?" Whispered a single neon whom was presently staring into George's unfocused eyes.

"Yes, what are you doing here, George? "Why are you not at home?" Came a louder voice.

"What are you doing, George? Go on tell us. Go on," Came another.

"Yeh, we don't mind you being here, George, but what are you up to, ehh?"

In various configurations, this simple question was repeated several more times by the many tiny iridescent red and blue neon fish, that appearing from nowhere, had suddenly enveloped George in a fishy flashing cloud. These fishes, known to be happy fish, were all smiling at him nose first, and speaking in unison:

"Tell us George... Please, why don't you."

"Yeh, why are you here, George?"

"Tell us, go on - *go on!*"

"Go away, you lot. I'm thinking," George declared, patiently.

Now, such a reply is a little thoughtless in itself, because it invites an understandable response that negates any request for privacy, in other words, it is asking for trouble.

"What are you thinking, George?"

"Yeh, what are you thinking, George? Tell us."

"Go on, tell us, George."

"George…"

These questions became unrelenting, until George abandoned any attempt at contemplation and snapped, "WILL YOU LOT PLEASE SHUT UP?!"

This sudden outburst, from what was considered a usually mild-mannered guppy, shocked the throng, who at once, shot away a good five centimetres, turned collectively, and stared right back at George, still smiling, yet puzzled.

"Sorry, I'm sorry, I didn't mean to frighten you," George said, repenting, "I'll tell you, if you all promise to listen and not speak all at once."

"We promise," came the unified response.

The multitude moved a little closer, eyes wide, expectant.

"Does any one of you ever wonder where you came from, why you are here, and once scooped up in The Net, where you are ultimately going to end up?"

For an instant the school exchanged bemused glances, and then replied, again in blissful harmony, *"No!"*

"Oh, you're like all the rest, hopeless..." George stated, as he turned and swam away.

"What's the matter with him?" asked a passing cichlid.

"I don't think that he is really a guppy," a neon, volunteered, "I think that he is lost soul – soul - sole - get it, you lot..."

Infectious laughter rippled among the multitude before they all moved off together, sniggering, in search of some other fish to pester.

*

In the confines of the fish tank passing the time was a popular pastime!? One particular fish - the pink, almond-shaped, kissing gourami - *let's name her Freda*, considered that her primary task in life was to complete as many laps of the fish tank that was fishily possible, beginning when The Light was first illuminated until it became extinguished again.

Neglected when a tiny tiddler, Freda loved adoration, and wanted desperately to appear in the Gudgeon Book of Fish Tank Records, and consequently, feel important. The present record was one thousand and ten laps, and held by a neon fish. Freda's record stood at thirty eight laps, which wasn't much, but Freda swam rather leisurely, and kept on being distracted from her task by her amorous nature.

"Freda, can I ask you something, please. A pressing question that has been taxing my brain?" George inquired, cruising up beside her.

"Fancy a snog?" Freda suggested hopefully, having not understood a word George had uttered and completing lap twenty-seven.

"NO, no. That's not what I want, at all!" George quickly stated.

"Ohhh... That's not nice," Freda said, retracting her sensuous pout and coming to a hurt stop, *"Why not* kiss me? There is nothing *better* to do around here."

"Sorry, I didn't mean to be rude, Freda. You are very attractive, it's just that I'm having a very bad day," George, confessed.

"*Mmmm,* ok... tell me about it." Freda curled her upper lip in response, ready to listen.

Now, what Freda was displaying by her resigned expression, was that she understood all about bad days, and had had quite enough of them in her life, and that she did not really want an explanation of George's malaise – However, Freda wasn't doing anything else worthwhile presently, and considering that due to her inactivity, todays record attempt was now beyond reach, she thought that she may as well listen...

"Go on then, ask away..." Freda said, in acquiescence.

George's response was immediate - "Freda, do you ever wonder about the meaning of life?"

Before replying, Freda deliberated for a while - *"Sometimes…"*

In response to this unexpected encouraging response, George processed too much water, *"GULP! COUGH!* "YOU DO!"

"Yep!"

"…and...?"

"And *what?*"

"What do you think the meaning of life is?"

"I think that everything just happens," Freda, mused.

George began to feel heartened, "Yes, yes, but *who,* or what, makes it happen?"

"Nobody, nothing, it just happens," Freda, murmured unhurriedly.

"That makes no sense - if you don't mind me saying," George said, pulling a face.

"I suppose that I'm a fishiest!" Freda said, emphatically elaborating.

"A fishiest – one of those fish that believe that nothing. Nothing at all made all of this." George held up his pectoral fins in astonishment, "You and me, the golden castle. Nothing created it? But the fish tank is beautiful, it can't have just happened in a big splash, like some say. It makes no sense at all. How then did the big splash happen? Explain that if you can!"

"Why not a big splash, it's as good an explanation as any other." Freda mused, "Well, that's what I think, anyway. What do you think, then, clever blup?"

George frowned, "I'm confused. One minute I believe The Big Fish exists, then I become a doubter, again, but only for a few days... and then I get to thinking he might not be real... Then I believe again. I suppose that I'm an agcodstic. You know - not certain if The Big Fish exists or not, but there must be something out there, don't you think?!"George's red eyes went out of focus and he seemed to go into a trance.

Freda pouted, "Cyril the crab is convinced that everything started with a flood!" Freda added, wistfully, "But he walks sideways…"

"I see…" George was still daydreaming.

"Mmmm… sure you don't fancy a snog, George?" Freda said, brightening.

George snapped out of it, "No, not today, thank you, Freda, I better be off."

"Well, please yourself. Bye then," Freda said, blowing a bubble kiss and commencing lap whatever (she had lost count and decided that the rest of the day would be spent in circuit training).

Returning to where Fred was sucking the life out

of gravel fragment three hundred-and-ninety-one since morning. George rested upon the bottom of the fish tank and began mindlessly observing him, exhausted by his fruitless quest.

"No-one is interested. They just don't seem to care," George said to himself, as Fred sucked on his booty. "What is the point of worrying, we will all find out one day, I suppose?"

Above and around George swam lots of fish. Some fish were resting upon the bottom of the fish tank, others were browsing here and there, one or two were amusing themselves play-fighting, a few were bored, being born, dying, lonely, ill, sad, or happy, and like George, some were not content. So it is true to say that existence in the fish tank was continuing as was considered normal.

"What's the matter with you, George?" asked Fred, spitting out a blue fragment of processed gravel that almost hit George's nose, "You look sad, lad."

"*I don't know* – I need to know if The Big Fish exists, or not, Fred..." George stared at Fred, pleadingly.

"Oh, cheer up and forget about it. Help me sieve this lot. We are all going into The Net some time or another, why worry about it?"

"Because I do. That's why!" George was

becoming upset, "If there is a heaven in the hood then I want to go to it, and some fish say naughty fish aren't allowed in. I'm not getting any younger, am I".

"Well, you're not old!" Fred said, encouragingly, "Look, George, you are not a bad fish," Fred lowered his head slightly, "Unlike some around here that I could mention - I'm sure that if The Big Fish exists then he will let you in to wherever he is. I would!

"You are very kind, Fred. But sometimes I tell little lies, and I once borrowed some especially pretty gravel and forgot to give it back, that's stealing, and it says in the deep sea scrolls that liars and thieves will not be allowed into the golden kingdom." George appeared really troubled.

"It wasn't any of my gravel, was it?" Fred appeared, slightly ruffled "No, no, it was some of the Generalists' gravel. That makes it worse!"

"Oh, stop worrying about things that don't matter. If The Big Fish is as kind as some say that he is, then he will forgive you," Fred said, emphatically.

"I'm not so sure, I read in the deep sea scrolls that 'Mercy cannot rob justice', and it says somewhere else that The Big Fish is a Just fish, so he can't just let me off - it says so in the scrolls, and rules are rules." George was certain.

"The scrolls, the scrolls. What good are the scrolls? You are getting far too clever for your own good. Stop reading such rubbish, it's turning your mind." Fred was getting aggravated. This conversation was getting far too deep for him.

"I might have to pay a fine for being bad and I don't have any fish food for payment, so I might end up in the fishy prison in the hood." George's mind was beginning to scramble.

"Who's told you that rubbish. A fishy prison in the hood? That's a lot of nonsense, George, "Why don't you visit a mind-doctor, perhaps he can help you," Fred suggested in desperation.

"It can't all be nonsense, some of it must be true, and I don't need a doctor, thanks, I need answers." George shed a tear, although Fred could not know because the tear drop became instantly diluted.

"Well, please yourself," Fred said, resuming his endless task of filtration.

Nevertheless, anxious for some peace of mind George took Fred's advice and through his GP (Genial Piscatorial), an eel, he made an appointment to consult Dr Ruffa, a cyprinid fish. A bearded fish who specialised in pontificating, hoodwinking, netting, gravel digging, and such related stuff.

*

Adhering upside-down to a decorative rock, Dr

Ruffa had a dimpled green and yellow face that displayed little emotion, yet somehow he managed to appear patient and kind. Relaxing under the doctor's head upon the pink sandy bed of the fish tank, George was staring upward with his eyes closed.

"Please go ahead," the doctor indicated with a fin.

George began explaining his state of mind. It took a while...

Dr Ruffa listened attentively, occasionally writing something in the sand with one of his sharp fins. Now and again George would stop blupping, open his eyes, and glance up in the doctor's direction to confirm that the doctor remained awake. Dr. Ken Ruffa *was* conscious, but struggling...

"'Please, do go on," the doctor, said, noticing George's sudden hard stare.

George did go on ....and on, and on, and on... taking the opportunity of explaining in great detail his theory concerning reality, existentialism, postmodernism, and the meaning of fishy life.

To signal the end of the session Dr Ruffa, stirred, stretched his fins, and smiled a benign smile, the way some doctor's do when they want to get rid of someone.

"You'll be fine... Try not to think about things too

much, old chap," The doctor suggested.

"That's it, Doc?" George said, confused all the more, "That's all that you have to say to me?"

"*Mmmm…*" Dr Ruffa confirmed, "And be sure to have a brisk swim each day, and eat lots of fresh waterweed."

Preserved in the sand until it was deleted by a wandering sponge, Dr. Ruffa's report was perused by George's slippery GP. It read as follows:

'<u>George Guppy:</u> Well presented, and eloquent. A very amiable but troubled immature fish.

<u>Diagnosis:</u>   Religious   mania.   Paranaoia. Generalised Pisces psychosis, and Rudd reality delusion.

<u>Probable Cause</u>: An absence of paediatric parental guidance, compounded by a lack of social confidence, accompanying an acute personality disorder, obfuscated by melancholy.

<u>Treatment</u>: Untreatable'.

*

In the fish tank talking to The Big Fish was uncommon, and to avoid ridicule, done quietly and in secret by only a few sincere believers. In fish parlance this activity was known as 'raying', but I will refer to it as praying. One morning, as if by chance, George encountered a rock fish named Rocky *(well, what did you expect?)* mumbling behind a rock. He appeared to be speaking to no one in particular, and seemed a likely candidate for Dr. Ruffa.

"What are *you* up to?" George asked, neon style, wondering if like himself, his knobbly friend was also losing his grip upon aquatic reality.

"I'm praying to The Big Fish in the hood - I'm not ashamed to admit it!" Rocky was quick to confirm.

"If he exists?" George muttered, disparagingly.

"He certainly does!" Rocky confirmed, adamantly.

"Are you sure about that?" George said, cynically.

"Well, there is only one way for you to find out!" Rocky announced, placing his long pectoral fins together and staring George in the eye.

"What, me, pray?" George said, incredulously, "Come on now...".

"And why not, I have heard tell that you have been asking searching questions about The Big Fish all over the place. Been causing rather a stir, you have - and if you really want to know, I was praying for you!"

"Err, well thanks anyway, but I don't need praying

for," George said, flustered, and embarrassed"...I'd feel stupid praying. It would be like talking to myself."

For a while no one spoke. George pretended to examined some gravel. Wearing a gentle smile Rocky gazed at George for what seemed ages.

In the end, George broke the silence, "What is the point of praying, Rocky, if there is a Big Fish he isn't going to speak to the likes of us, is he..."

"He speaks to me, George - *maybe not in words*, but he does," Rocky said, "Why don't you give it a try, are you too proud, what have you got to lose?"

George was not proud, well, perhaps a little, but he *was* sceptical. Praying seemed a delusionary practice, like requesting to be fooled.

"The Big Fish is always listening! Rocky said.

"Is he? All right, then Rocky – tell me, what do you think life is all about, existence, The Net, all that stuff, I can't make any sense out of it," George asked, then wished that he hadn't.

Rocky's expression became intent, "George, what you need is faith, not facts. It is written in the deep sea scrolls that 'Wise men will become fools, and fools will become wise'."

George was getting irritated, "I've also read it -

else all the bad fishes would not need faith in order to believe, and that would not be a good thing, right?"

Yes, that's correct. Do you really want to know the truth, George. Are you ready to listen to the good news?"

George thought for a minute... "No, not at the moment, perhaps later. Sorry..." George said, apologetically, feeling uncomfortably self-conscious.

Ignoring George's protestations, and keen to be a do-gooder, Rocky began to sermonise - a bad idea: "The fish tank was once *extremely* beautiful, clean and pure - as The Big Fish always intended it to be. He created it that way so that we fish might all live together with him contentedly, forever, without going motionless. But we fish were led astray by a selfish, lying, sea snake, and we did bad things, so that it was impossible for The Big Fish, who is perfect, kind, just, and good, to live with us."

Wishing that he could turn tail and swim away but too polite to do so, George was not listening. His eyes began to glaze over as Rocky filled his gills for a second time and continued:

"So The Big Fish swam away promising to come back sometime, leaving the wicked sea snake to do his thing. That's when the water began to turn foggy and instead of living forever, we fish began to go motionless..."

"...Rocky, why do you believe all that weird stuff?" George said, interrupting the diatribe, and twisting his mouth in disbelief.

"I have prayed about it."

"Oh... that explains it, then" George said, sighing, certain that Rocky had swallowed too many bubbles.

"So," Rocky continued, whether George wanted to listen or not. "A lot later on The Big Fish, sent The Son Fish - as he had promised previously. The Son Fish offered to take the blame for all the bad things that we fish had done. This made it possible for we who believe in The Son Fish, to eventually enter the wonderful place in the hood where The Big Fish and The Son Fish rule together.

Another embarrassing silence followed where Rocky gazed at George to determine if the good news was having any effect. It was, but not the impact Rocky had hoped for. To George, this story sounded farfetched - Rocky bubbled on annoyingly:

"When The Son Fish did come back the bad fish did not recognise him, they got cross and told him to stop talking rubbish and to go away. When he did not go away, and kept making motionless fish move again, and curing sick fish, they got even madder and took him away and hurt him badly. They stuck sharp hooks into him and hung him up outside the golden castle until he started to bleed from lots of wounds and the water turned crimson. Then he stopped moving...

George had heard enough, and unexpectedly his patience smothered his kindness. Before he could stop himself, he said what he was thinking, "Please, shut up, Rocky," George uttered, "You sound like that long-finned, black and white, female disc fish. Instantly George regretted what he had said, but the words had escaped and could not be recaptured, "Sorry, Rocky..." George, said, contritely.

"No, I got carried away, it's my fault, young kipper, no hard feelings. Perhaps I will see you at old Eeelies goodbye gathering?"

"Yeah, maybe," George replied, as they parted.

3 FOLLOWERS

Akin to Rocky, among the fishy community it was common knowledge that the long-finned, black and white, disc fish, considered that she was hatched again. An Angelavist. This stunning, graceful, and mysterious fish, was large, solitary, and also tended to disappear and appear at odd times and in odd places. She could usually be found habituating a top corner of the fish tank, just beneath the surface, gazing up into glassy space as if expecting someone. Let's name her Angel.

Angel was a loner and being a self-taught deep sea scroll reading Angelavist, did not belong to any particular school of fishes of faith, such as the Batholics. She informed all that wanted to know that she believed that The Son Fish had volunteered to be, caught, wounded, and made motionless before being taken away by The Net. Most fishes of faith considered Angel's beliefs extreme and avoided her. She was obviously abnormal.

The Batholics morphed into existence in the distant past, sometime after The Son Fish had departed into the hood, and they had drawn to themselves a large school of traditional fishy adherents. Most Batholics attended fish faith meetings because their parents did, or had, and would teach their tiddlers likewise, it was traditional!

Batholics, were supposed to be very strict, and members had to do as they were told, and believe what they were told. The leaders tended to be all male and had to live their whole life without a partner. Something George could not understand, because he knew that it was not good to be alone.

If a Batholic was ever naughty, which each was, in order to remain a Batholic in good standing, and not end up in a muddy puddle for all eternity, then they had to own-up and say sorry in secret to a hidden leader at the very next meeting. Every so often a Batholic had to do a forfeit In order to be forgiven, like repeating a prayer word for word, or having to sift some gravel whilst praying. If they did not come clean they were destined to a muddy puddle forever. Which was very scary and frightened a lot of Batholics into obedience. Unless they stayed at home that week and didn't bother going to the meeting.

The Batholics assembled within the bubbling golden castle, every seventh day. Over eons the castle had been decorated with all kinds of shiny fishy symbols, sand sculptures, and twinkling representations of tiny fishing nets. Here and there could be found pretty mounds of sorted gravel, selected shells, and water weed displays. It was felt that ostentation was very important. George did not know why this was so, and wondered what The Big Fish thought about it, if he existed, that is...

However, George realised that a lot of Batholics who regularly attend the meetings and prayed a lot, at other times, spent their days in naughty fish tank distractions, such as fighting, stealing fish food, saying bad words, or pursuing the partners of other fishes. They were not stupid fishes, but rather clever fishes, they realised that if they secretly said sorry at the next meeting then they would be forgiven, so all was well, wasn't it...

The other large group of faith fishes in the fish tank, were the Generalists. They taught that as long as you believed in some power or other beyond the hood, and tried to do your best, then everything would turn out for the best. Their teaching were a bit vague and some contradictory, but even though divided in some doctrinal beliefs, they did agreed on one thing - that when you stopped moving The Net would spirit you away to meet The Big Fish, or several Big Fish, or some fish like The Big Fish?

The Generalists also felt that after you had succumbed to motionless that you would end up someplace wonderful and not down in the mud, and that The Big Fish would forgive bad Generalists of everything, because he loved everyone unconditionally!

Nice fishes, The Generalist leaders were not even

upset if you failed to attend meetings. It was not surprising therefore that they did not have any firm answers to George's earnest questions!

George wasn't drawn to the Generalist, the Batholic, or the Angelavist creed, to him none made any sense. However, one thing George deemed was true, was that most faith fishes seemed, if rather self-righteous, to be affable friendly fish, which to them seemed to be the most important thing all...

The appearance of The Net usually coincided with the disappearance of yet another elderly or sick fish, customarily one of the faith leaders would hold a netting service and deliver a practiced and familiar homily. They did this so that the faith fishes might pray, blub, and remember the departed affectionately, but mostly to feel good about themselves.

Being gregarious, George attended the occasional netting meeting, and had tolerated varied traditional discourses on the matter of life after the fish tank. Good-naturedly, George had listened to long, and exhaustive portrayals of the lives of now motionless members, some delivered by leaders who got their facts wrong, having never actually known the departed! This was always amusing, annoying, or frustrating, depending on a relationship point of view. It was also notable that positive fishy traits of the motionless were ever exaggerated and negative ones were never mentioned.

Now and again, relatives of the netted who were unbelievers, would hold a 'celebration of life' meeting even if the dear departed had been the most boring fish in the fish tank? Later they would all get together and say nice things about the departed fish, and suck gravel, it made them all feel happy at what should have been a sad time. Very odd, thought George...

Netting ceremonies conducted by Loofarian leaders, fierce looking fish with white necks, were accompanied by much fin waving, wild eyes, spluttering, and a mighty blupping. This reaction could be taken as a very edifying sermon, an entertaining performance, or rather tedious, either way. However, it was generally accepted by attendees that the departed had gone to a better place – this location was a great mystery to all, but it was explained by those who knew everything that in the fullness of time - whenever that was supposed to be, that any outstanding ambiguities would be understood?

Contrasting with the more consolatory and relaxed netting ritual of the Generalist group, the Batholics ceremony lasted forever, seemed stricter, was conducted with much pomp, and seemed at times weird. Also the Batholic observations contained obscure customs, and rather than clarifying existence, stirred the water into a cloud with their out-gushing's and veiled threats, tending to make George cough, rather than convincing him of anything.

According to Batholic tradition, apparently George was going to suffer everlasting punishment in the mud, unless he became a Batholic and began doing as he was told. Nevertheless, this nebulous elucidation at netting services seemed to satisfy the compliant mass of Batholics, who felt reassured that all was well in the fish tank, before going home to continue being naughty.

Oh, there was another group of faith fish named the Friendly Fish, they were once very nervous fish and used to shake fearfully when anyone mentioned The Big Fish. Their meetings were mostly silent and not a lot happened, so George never attended.

Then there was the Hoodists, they believed that after a fish had been taken by The Net, no matter what kind of fish that it was, it would later be reintroduced back into the tank as a different kind of species, depending on its departed moral status. Such as a shrimp, or a catfish, or a dogfish - something. Water fleas - who were at the bottom of the top one hundred pecking list, considered that this belief was wonderful, because their chances of coming back as something bigger and better were very good indeed, but giant guppies were not so keen. George, a small guppy, considered this absurd conviction spoke for itself.

What other group was there? Let's not forget the sundry faith fishes that worshiped hundreds of different kinds of The Big Fish. Fish-made idols in all colours, shapes and sizes. Bits of gravel stuck together with snail cement. A blue rock, a pretty piece of weed - just to make certain that they had not overlooked an unknown Big Fish, and had covered all their options – yes, that made sense?

Or the violent fishes that pretended to believe in peace. The ones that worshiped a particular blood thirsty Big Fish. The Big Fish who they considered to be the greatest of all The Big Fishes, whose members considered that it was a virtue to kill other fishes who did not worship him, or behave the way that they did.

And then there was the scattered separatist fishes that always massed together and seemed to belong nowhere. They were bullied a lot and few fishes accepted or wanted them in their territory. These separatists appeared different, and had been taught from the beginning of the fish tank that they were the Chosen Fishes and that The Big Fish belonged to them alone. They were waiting for the promised Son Fish who would rescue them and become their king fish, but he had not come as yet, but they were ever hopeful.

It was known that some migratory fish followed a school that taught polack-amy, thus many female fish shared but one partner and bred lots of tiddlers. These faith fishes also hoarded fish food so that they might have something to eat when, fish food would cease to arrive in the last days, and the water would become so cloudy that surviving fish would not be able see forward at all. They maintained that unbelievers would starve into motionless before The Son Fish could come back to save but them!

Another odd group, who went under the name of Wetnesses, followed teachers who had rewritten the deep sea scrolls to suit their own theories. The Wetnesses interpreted the new translations by committee before deciding what was sensible to be taught to followers as being true. They swam in pairs going from weed to weed looking for converts and annoying everyone.

The fish tank was becoming crazier than ever.

But above all this insanity, the one thing that annoyed George the most, was - how come most of the faith leaders lived in comfort, whilst many of the fish in the fish tank were starving?

So there we have it, is it any wonder that George was confused and thought that, along with the majority of the free-thinking free-swimming fish in the fish tank, that all of The Big Fish worshipers were bonkers, and the main cause of every violent dispute that had ever taken place in the fishy abode since time began.

Floating high above, Angel, did not get involved in the conflict, but just smiled to herself.

4 CLOUDS

The outlook was not clear, because the water in the fish tank was cloudier than was usual. The mighty depletion of the water and the replenishing whoosh, was occurring less and less frequently, and some of the fish were worried that if this state of affairs continued, then the end of the fish tank could be coming sooner than later, and so they prayed more frequently.

Others couldn't care less and stirred up the water even more, just to be awkward.

Certain young fishy environmentalists popularised the notion that The Light in the hood was getting hotter due to The Net dropping water upon it less often. This increase in hood induction had caused flaked fish food to condense into clumps that dissolved slower in the water than in the past. Obviously a nebulous chain reaction was occurring and the water was becoming thicker each day. When consulted about this proven fact, it gave these fishes a grand feeling of self-importance and extra fish food. Whilst munching they explained that, alas nothing could be done about it, and it was up to The Big Fish to sort it out.

Some very confident fish preached that the problem of water pollution was due to heating glass change, or caused by fish tank warming, Fred's fish gravel disturbance, or some such thing, and all fishes should do something about it at once. Such as eating less, staying asleep longer, killing Fred, or should not become born at all!

Scabby looking aquatic environmentalists tended to believe in abstaining from eating ant's eggs, or unnatural fish flakes, and with pale gills, they tended to live solely on waterweed. This peculiarity annoyed the milling neon fish, whom did not like it when their home was being devoured.

Also being polackitly correct, most fishy environmentalists did not believe in the existence of The Big Fish, and collectively referred to their fellow environmentalists as 'Fish Tank Savers'. Their intent was to rescue the fish tank from certain disaster, by holding regular noisy and disruptive meetings.

All these environmentalists generally made a sanctimonious nuisance of themselves, but in the minority, few fish were brave enough to disagree with them, including George.

*

Fish tank tradition had it that in a gargantuan fish tank elsewhere, a massive sea-creature named a whale, had once accidently swallowed a drowning organism named a Jonah - a creature that had legs where its fins should be. A few days later the whale regurgitated the Jonah, whereupon the whale conducted an interesting conversation with him.

The whale reiterated his encounter with Jonah to a shoal of nosy pilchards, who later told a passing squid the tale, who informed a migrating salmon of all the facts, who whispered to a meandering fresh-water shrimp the details. He, one day, to his surprise, found himself in the present fish tank without a clue concerning how he got there, but with a perfect recollection of Jonah's mishap.

Thereafter this fresh-water shrimp explained to any fish that would listen, that the partly digested Jonah being, had articulated to the whale that he knew for a fact that The Big Fish was real. It also transpired that by not following The Big Fish's instructions in the first place, the finless creature had got itself into a lot of trouble, and this was the cause of the whale's indigestion. An entertaining aside, most fishes supposed, but a bonkers fable nevertheless.

However, despite Rocky's confirmation that the Jonah story was written in the deep sea scrolls,

George couldn't be bothered to search for it.

The fresh-water shrimp believed some other odd stories, like - the cause of regular fish tank darkness was the effect of mass temporary hallucinatory blindness, and nothing to do with The Light. A blindness that occurred simultaneously at the end of each fishy day. An affliction that lasted for a varying period of time until eyesight suddenly returned in the morning. Experts said that this phenomenon, and fish tank warming were proven facts, so it was true.

*

Over time the water in the fish tank had grown increasingly cloudy, and unable to see but for a few centimetres ahead, George swam cautiously.

As we have learnt, some fish believed that the fact that the water in the fish tank was getting rather warmer and cloudier than was usual, was a sign of the times, whatever time that was? George was not certain about that, but proceeding with care, he nevertheless nearly bumped into a slimy loach, which was not a pleasant experience!

Further on, as George was carefully side-swimming, to avoid the gaping mouth of a very big gobbling- predatory bass, who was searching for its lunch, and had identified George as a candidate, when a slight fish tank shaking sensation could be felt.

Rapidly the tremor increased until the whole fish tank started to vibrate, and in varying degrees of fear and excitement, all the fish panicked at once, including George, who made for a top corner of the fish tank to try to escape the swaying sloshing of the water.

After a while things began to return to normal, and all was calm, it was then decided by the faith fishes that more praying was required to try to appease The Big Fish.

This decision started an argument between the Generalists, the Chosen Fishes, and the Batholics, concerning which group should predominately pray in the golden castle, and an unholy brawling broke out.

In an attempt at peacekeeping the blue headed United Species Organisation (plaice keeping group), tried to separate the factions by spitting gravel at the main protagonists. The main protagonists hit back by stirring up the sand and flipping pretty pebbles at them.

In the cloud of pink sand, and flipped projectiles feisty fish were fighting all over the place.

To George there seemed to be no reason for all the bad feeling. As if something malicious that could not be seen was stirring anger into the pollution.

Before The Light went out that day all sides grew

tired of fighting, and calling a truce, decided to have a prayer rota, then they all swam home to have a rest.

When the water finally whooshed, in the morning and all was clear, many prayers were said in thankfulness. But hidden behind the castle George discovered a stockpile of big pebbles.

Whenever the fish tank shook, which was taking place more frequently than was ever, the water in the fish tank swilled all about in an alarming fashion, and things that were usually static shifted position.

On one occasion the golden castle toppled right over, causing bursting bubbles to pop everywhere, terrifying the General followers.

Thankfully, from out of nowhere The Net suddenly materialised, plunged deep into the water, and somehow righted the castle, restoring calm. A miracle! Or was it?

The Generalists believed that miracles did not happen anymore, and that the appearance of The Net was just a coincidence.

The leader of the Batholics stated that a water changing tsunami was not a sign of the times, as some had erroneously supposed, but that these things had always happened, and always would. It was nothing to be concerned about. But it did prove that this event was a clear sign from The Big Fish that the golden castle belonged to his lot.

But George was not so sure…

These mixed groups of praying fishes were becoming bothersome.

*

Angel was swaying gently, her gaze focused upon the hood, as looking in the opposite direction, George gently collided with her.

"Sorry, Angel, I was looking out for the gobbling-bass. A bit unexpected that tsunami the other day, wasn't it. Do you believe it was a sign of the times, as most fishes of faith seem to think? "

Angel lowered her eyes and stared at George, which was somewhat disconcerting, "Before the end of the fish tank comes about, there are much worse calamities to endure, George," Angel stated, emphatically.

George did not like that reply and tried to change the subject, "What are you looking at, Angel. You're always staring into space?" George, questioned, peering upwards.

"I'm not looking at, but for," Angel, clarified.

"What are you looking *for*, then, Angel?" George said.

"For the return of The Son Fish."

"Really. Why?" George sighed, bored with hearing the same old fishy story, but obliged to continue.

"Because I believe in him."

"What do you believe?" George looked fed up.

"I believe that The Son Fish is coming back to lead 'The Dash', and to save the fish tank."

"Oh yeah…" George remarked, cynically, "I've heard that fishy story before. Do you really believe it?"

Angel did not remove her gaze from the hood, "I don't believe it. I know it."

"Well... Good for you!" George, said.

George didn't mean to be rude, and bit his lip, but to his astonishment, Angel was not upset. She turned and smiled radiantly at him.

"These days, few fish believe in the return of The Son Fish, except me, and Rocky of course, and maybe you - one day!" Angel, said.

"I don't think so," George said, emphatically.

Angel looked momentarily wistful, "You never

know, George," she, said.

"I'm sorry, Angel. Everything is so mixed up. I don't know what I believe?" George stated, unhappily, "I try to be good, but it's impossible!"

George looked miserable, he hadn't smiled for days and days.

Angel looked straight into George's hooded eyes and a soft glow seemed to radiate from her face, "Listen to me, George - Despite what other fishes may say, The Big Fish is real, and I am looking forward to meeting his..."

"I know ...Son. I've heard it all so many times before. But you're not a bad fish, Angel. Whatever happens, you will definitely go to a better life in the hood."

"Mercy cannot rob justice, George. We have all done things wrong, sometime or another, including me, and wonderful you," Angel, said.

"I've heard that too... Just tell me, Angel, why is the fish tank made the way that it is?" George asked, "And what can be done about everything being in such a mess?"

Then, before George could ask another question, without warning the whoosh whooshed, Angel vanished, the water cleared miraculously, and all was forgotten for another few clear days.

5 QUESTIONS

The new fish that appeared unannounced in the fish tank one morning, seemed very odd. Very odd indeed. It was flat, it had one eye positioned upon the upper surface of its camouflaged body, and one eye set in its lower surface. This enabled the fish to see up and down at the same time, and when lying upon the bottom with one eye shut, not to be seen at all - a great advantage when seeking peace and quiet, or anonymity.

Yet despite these fine attributes, shy Mary's arrival had not gone unnoticed.

"You're new, aren't you?" The question came from Fred, the famous bottom feeder.

"How did you know where I was hiding?" Mary, whispered, surprised to be discovered.

"You're reposing upon my dinner," Fred, complained.

"Oh, I'm so sorry," Mary, exclaimed.

With a quick flap of her flat wings, Mary moved away a few centimetres, disturbing the gravel.

Fred re-positioned himself, and begin to sift a few fragments of discarded lunch that had been exposed at the base of the fish tank.

"Don't apologise, lass, you've done me a favour," Fred said, delighted to discover hidden foody treasures, "My names Fred, by the way."

"Nice to meet you Fred, my name's Mary. How does the food get here – I don't appear to know anything?" Mary asked as Fred ate, not an unreasonable question coming from a hungry fish.

"It comes from above, twice a day," Fred, informed Mary, "But don't worry, now that you are here, extra food will appear, automatically."

"How does *that* work?" Mary, asked, perplexed.

"I have not got a clue, it just happens, Fred said, "Tell me, where do you come from, Mary?"

Mary was pensive, "Like I said, I can't remember a thing…"

"No, none of us fish can remember where we come from, but I thought that I would ask you anyway. One never knows, you know."

Just then, on his non-stop circumnavigation around the fish tank, a flashing blue short finned shark swam close by, searching for a mouth-sized breakfast.

Fred quickly moved out of the way as the fish swept by, "Don't ever get in Micks way, he has a lot of sharp teeth, and he's not at all nice," Fred advised.

"I don't intend to get in anyone's way," Mary said, flapping away at a sedentary pace, "Goodbye, Fred, and thank you for taking the time to talk to me."

*

As we may have realised, Impulsiveness is not a part of George's nature, he tended to think a lot, perhaps too much, and he wasn't given to spontaneous action. But when for the first time he spotted half-hidden Mary, he felt a sudden urge to swim up to the attractive resting foreigner for a chat.

"Hello, my names George, why are you hiding, and what's your name?"

Now as an introductory gambit between tiddlers, this form of address is acceptable, in fact laudable. But for a growing male fish to use it, who is coloured yellow, with green spots, and has a big mouth, and appears above a growing female fish without any warning, it can understandingly cause alarm.

"AHHHHH…!" exclaimed Mary, as she flapped away in fear.

"Please don't go, I didn't mean to startle you. I only wanted to talk. I'm so sorry," George cried after her.

Remaining uncertain of George's motives, but determining that George seemed harmless, Mary decelerated and with her lower eye, looked back. George had stopped pursuing her, and seemed very contrite.

"For a second I thought that you were Mike, I've heard that he is nasty," Mary, revealed, ending her flight.

"No, no, I'm George – I'm nice, least I try to be, even though these days I don't smile that much," George said, with a slight blush, "I'm an agcodstic."

Why George blurted out this addition piece of unrequested information, puzzled them both.

"Oh, I'm a flatfish," Mary, confirmed.

"No, no, I'm a guppy, but…"

"You're confusing me," Mary said, appearing anxious.

"I'm an agcodstic…" George, added.

George was not getting through, and Mary gave him a very perplexed stare.

George tried to explain, "An agcodstic is a fish who believes that nothing is known, or can be known, of the existence, or nature, of The Big Fish. Most people think that an agcodstic isn't sure what to believe, but that's not true – Fred told me that, once."

This additional uninvited information caused Mary more unease, "I see…" Mary said – but she didn't.

"I think that Mike is an aseaist – you know, the type of fish that doesn't believe anything is up there." George lifted his head in an upward motion and gazed toward the top of the tank.

Awash with new facts, but sympathetic to George's malaise, Mary felt that she should at least state her conviction, "I'm not an anything. I don't think about such things. Polacktics and generalisation are best not discussed. It causes so much unrest in fish society, don't you think, George?"

It was at that precise juncture that Sam swam into

view. Sam was a yellow striped black red-eyed cichlid, and was very intelligent, or so he believed. Sam had an eye for the ladies, so it was not long before he smarmily introduced himself and, uninvited, joined in the discussion.

"They say that The Big Fish created this fish tank a short while ago, but this fish tank is ages old, Darling. Just examine the old green gunk over there, and look at the tiny shell fossils trapped in the ancient gravel. Anyone with half a brain can tell that this fish tank is very old, very, very, old, trillions of Lights old." With a smug expression, Sam indicated the bed of the fish tank. "Also, it takes real courage to understand that once you are motionless, then you are motionless. That's it is all over – forever!"

Shocked, sensitive Mary looked upset, "Then what is the point of existence?" Mary wanted to know, one eye going from one fish to the other.

George began to get excited, "Yes," George, chipped in, staring at Sam, "What *is* it all about?"

"There isn't any point to it, at all," Sam pompously stated, "That's the point! That's why I became a fishiest," he said, with a lofty air, seemingly quite proud of his considered superior intellectual position in believing in nothing at all.

This statement did not satisfy George, who went into contemplation mode - The big question remained, just how did the fish tank come into being? If it was made, what, or who made it, how was it made, and why? George pondered.

"What about the existence of The Big Fish that I have been hearing about?" Mary, asked.

Sam shook his head, "Only foolish creatures believe in The Big Fish. Weak fish. Those that need something to hang on to. Kid yourself if you must, but as for me I am not that stupid," Sam stated, categorically, "I'm a wise guy! Laws were made to keep us in our place and allow cleverer fish to break them, get away with it, and dominate."

Mary did not take too well to the insinuation that she was perhaps weak, or stupid, "Well... I think that truth is truth. The fish tank either was, or it wasn't created," Mary determined, "No-one can really say for certain, can they!"

"That's right, Mary," George agreed, warming to Mary's gentle nature, "What is truth, and how are we to recognise it, for certain?"

"Don't delude yourselves, for Light years greater fish than you or I have pondered that question, stop worrying about it you two. Life's too short."

'Light years was a new concept to both George and Mary, but before they could ask Sam to explain what it meant, Sam pulled another smug face and without saying goodbye, swam away into the shadows, and if a fish could have whistled, he would have.

6 ANSWERS

Just which particular bored fish suggested that it was about time that a party was organised, was not substantiated, but word soon got around that a get-together was to be held the next day, before the food shower occurred.

Now fishy parties are not the kind that we humans enjoy, no. They are very different. The Dash is the primary celebration activity, and is done en-mass.

Before the start of The Dash is signalled, all participants gather in a designated corner of the fish tank, and then at a prearranged signal - they dash. The dash in the same direction attempting to keep in one body of fish, following whatever fish takes and can keep the lead, but taking *no particular* bearing. This madness continues until the food shower occurs, which can take a while.

Notably, The Dash seems to prompt a larger food shower than is usual, as if boosting the feeding occurrence. Once the food appears, a particularly feverish gobbling commences, until not a scrap of sustenance remains.

However, the reason that a party is decided upon is usually the same excuse as we humans employ – a birthday, an auspicious occasion, a celebration, etc. etc. As to whether or not the subject of the merriment manages to obtain any nutrition in the food free-for-all, does not seem to matter a jot.

This particular dashing excuse was a birthday. Old Tom was selected as the most ancient fish in the fish tank, hence his name. As far as anyone could ascertain, tomorrow he had been around for thirteen years, or near enough.

It was considered to be a great honour to be chosen to signal the start of The Dash, and to his horror, Fred was selected. He was terrified because he knew that he had to indicate 'The Off' by floating upside down upon the surface of the fish tank motionless for a while. Fred also understood that he had to remain inert until The Net appeared under the surface, and then to suddenly come to life and speed away out of The Nets reach. A risky business!

Sure enough, as fish eggs are bubbles, when the appointed time grew near, Fred was nowhere to be found!

"What you doing, Fred?" Inquired a neon.

"Yes, what you doing lurking in our waterweed, Fred?" Asked another.

"Go on tell us, Fred, what you doing here, are you hiding?" A load more tiny iridescent fish enquired, closing in on Fred, "Why aren't you signalling the start of The Dash, Fred?

Surrounded, Fred surrendered.

*

With great trepidation, Fred tried to relax, took a deep blup, and allowed his body to gravitate upwards…

Anticipating the imminent arrival of The Net, all the participating fish were gathered in a corner of the fish tank, watching Fred as he gradually neared the surface. They waited breathlessly, gills hardly moving, loitering in excitement, all beady-eyed and alert.

Motionless. Floating anxiously. Bubbles from the golden castle popping all around him, Fred lay upon the water and began to whisper a prayer, his red eyes open as wide as could be, his body inert, "Please, The Big Fish, if you are up there, keep me safe, and I promise I will be good for evermore, Amen."

Time slowed down and almost came to a halt.

Slowly drifting in the circular current upon the surface of the fish tank, Fred bobbed up and down. He hardly needed to act the part of a motionless fish - he was literally scared stiff!

Another age seemed to pass by, when swiftly a shadow crossed the sky and a flash of green appeared in the hood. Fred tensed. Then the darkened heavens reverberated with what sounded like sad rolling thunder.

Splosh!

The split-second The Net hit the water, Fred was away – shooting down toward the bottom of the fish tank as fast as his thrashing tail and thrusting fins could propel him. Down and down, down towards the welcoming depths of obscurity!

Also having avoided The Net, Angel was slowly circling beneath the surface of the fish tank, looking downward upon the proceedings, wearing a knowing expression.

A great cheer came from the mass of fish as Fred bounced off the bottom of the fish tank, and without further ado, The Dash commenced!

What fun it was, all the fish speeding in organised confusion in no particular direction. Round and around and up and down they went. From one side of the fish tank to the other. Suddenly coming to a halt, then changing track and speeding back. The murky water swirling and frothing, waterweed swaying in the tearing surge of the tumultuous tide of happy aquatics.

"HAPPY BLURPDAY TO YOU!" They all sang, together, "A HAPPY BLURPDAY TO YOU. A HAPPY BLURPDAY, DEAR OLD TOR-OORM. SWIM INTO THE BLUE!"

Grinning and blupping hard, Old Tom had recovered from his anxiety and was having a high old time, experiencing great excitement, the like of which he had never felt since he was a small fry.

Rejuvenated, Tom got his nose in front and led the mass for a while, before being overtaken by some enthusiastic neon about a tenth his age. It was amazing that in all the exhilaration not one fish collided with another.

After several minutes of this mad activity, the water was less than clear, and all were beginning to get fatigued. So it was with some relief, when a more sizable than was usual amount of fish flakes began to settle upon the choppy surface of the fish tank.

"GRUB UP, EVERYONE!" An unknown fish blupped at the top of his gills, espying the feast.

The Dash did one last dash to the surface, and a frenzied feeding began.

It wasn't long before all of the fish food had vanished. Then one by one, the gratified crowd gravitated to their individual style of habitation. Fred to his gravel sifting - having totally forgotten his prayer to The Big Fish, Mary to her graceful meandering. Mick to being dangerous. George to being troubled, and the neons to being nosey. Yes, life in the fish tank soon returned to normal.

*

Valuing Old Toms sagacity, and remaining desperately in need of an answer to the meaning of life, George wanted to ask Old Tom a pressing question about pre-existence, but since The Dash Old Tom had disappeared. Now there was only so many places to hide in the fish tank and George methodically visited each one.

The first place that George looked was among the swaying waterweed where the neons hung out, you can imagine that he had plenty of assistance for that search. Then he hunted around and about the golden castle, then in various dark corners, amongst the coloured gravel, and behind the heating element. George searched everywhere without success!

George asked everyone that he met as to Old Tom's whereabouts. The Wetnesses were most helpful, but got in the way, and wanted to talk about salvation rather than Old Tom. Some fish were not cooperative, and a few said that they saw him early that morning, others last night, but not a kipper had seen him recently. Old Tom remained nowhere to be found!

In despair George raised his eyes up to the heavens. And there he saw Old Tom floating upon the surface of the water, upside down and motionless. And what Old Tom was signalling, was not the beginning of another Dash, but that his body was waiting for The Net to take him to meet The Big Fish in the hood.

As George wept, his tears dissolving in the murky water, he swam up to the top of the fish tank and slowly circled around lifeless Old Tom, unafraid that any second he too might be netted along with his fishy friend.

Below, sighting the green shadow of The Net approaching the two fish, the body of fish panicked, and scattered in all directions, but George remained calm.

Sad thunder rolled, The Net plunged into the water, just missing George, and dripping aquatic droplets that resembled tears from heaven, The Net spirited Old Tom away.

*

Over the following months the sploshing of The Net and the whooshing of the water became less frequent. The Light stayed out for days at a time, the fish food came spasmodically, and the water became chillier. Subsequently the water became green and murky, and the fish surviving were ever hungry, miserable, and argumentative, Including

George – but especially the fish of faith. Only Angel remained smiling.

*

It took an age before the departure of Old Tom faded away into the majority of fishy memories, and it was a while before Mary felt that she might be able to approach George with a word or two of consolation.

Searching in the gloom, Mary discovered the sad and depressed young guppy occupying a quiet corner of the fish tank.

"What do you want, Mary?" George was feeling sorry for himself.

"I thought that you might like to talk," Mary said, gently, "You were very fond of Old Tom, weren't you…"

"Why do you want to know?" George snapped.

"I'm sorry, I'll go away." Mary stuttered, blushing and appearing hurt.

Unsmiling, George said nothing and Mary began to swim away.

"George suddenly realised that he was being cruel, and blurted out an apology, "Sorry, Mary, please come back. It's just that, just that... I don't know…"

Mary turned around and settled beside tearful

George, "Well, perhaps he's better off now, up in the hood. He was very old," Mary, added, "...and he had lots of aches and pains, they say."

George shook his head in a - 'I don't really know', fashion. Painful memories returned, "Old Tom never harmed anyone. Why did he have to go motionless? Is he up in the hood, or just gone? I don't understand, anything, Mary," George volunteered, "I was once told that all you had to do to never go motionless was to pray to The Big Fish, be sincerely sorry for all that you had done wrong, and then miraculously, you would be hatched again, and became a new fish - How's that work?"

Mary looked down, "It works by having faith, I believe," she said, "Least that's what Angel says."

"I wish that I did believe!" George, declared.

"Then why don't you give faith a try?" Mary suggested, brightening, "What have you to lose?"

George went into withdrawal again. Silent, Mary remained at his side.

A minute or two later, emanating from somewhere up above, Angel materialised, and after greeting Mary, turned her attention to George.

"Yes, why not give faith a try, George?" Angel said, smiling.

"How did you know what we are talking about?" George asked, puzzled.

"Oh, a little neon told me," Angel replied, her eyes sparkling.

George was no further forward in his quest for answers, in fact he felt that he was back at the start again. He felt so disheartened that he had run out of questions. George saw little point in living, nor could he make any sense of all the differing explanations for existence. Life was what it was, not what he wanted it to be. All around him was evidence that the fish tank was in a chaos, and getting worse, and that the majority of the fish swimming in the increasing filth were impatient, proud, selfish, self-obsessed, mean, lawless, and unhappy. Life was not fair, fish were being victimised, the weak were suffering, and the hungry were starving. The bad fish were prospering, the good fish were poor. If there was The Big Fish why did he allow such things to happen?

"I will leave you to think it over, George. Talk to you later," Angel could see that it was not the time for further conversation, and motioned to Mary.

"Ok, see you..." Mary said, her eyes as cloudy as the water.

The two fish swam into the darkness...

Off went The Light.

On went The Light.

'Whoosh' went the replenishment, as the level of the murky water gradually decreased, a little at a time.

In fell the fish food.

Off went The Light.

On went The Light.

'Whoosh' went the replenishment, as the level of the murky water gradually decreased, a little at a time.

In fell the fish food.

Off went The Light.

On went The Light.

'Whoosh' went the replenishment, as the level of the murky water gradually decreased, a little at a time.

In fell the fish food.

Off went The Light.

'Blup. Blup. Blup', went existence, a little at a time.

*

Innumerable on and offs later, one of the oldest fishes in the fish tank was looking upwards towards the hood and smiling to himself.

"What do you keep smiling at, Old George?" A young neon asked, puzzled by George's permanent demeanour."

"Do you really want to know?" George said...

7 WHAT GEORGE DISCOVERED

After studying the deep sea scrolls, and doing a lot of praying, this is what George believes to be true.

George will not bore you with scriptural references, lists of ancient texts, or literary works that support each of the convictions listed hereafter, after all, he is a fish and not an academic, and does not possess the intellect or the patience for that undertaking, but these sources do exist. Perhaps you might discover them for yourself? But remember, it does not matter a jot about whether some bible stories are metaphors or factual, or neither, it is the message that is important, and acting upon it.

*

WHO IS THE BIG FISH?

There is but one God.

God is a spirit, known in ancient texts as an 'elohim'. A name given to all disembodied spirits.

God has always existed. His name is 'YHWH' or 'I Am'. A name revealed to the prophet Moses by YHWH, using four Hebrew consonants. Probably pronounced – 'Yahweh'.

Yahweh God, has a heavenly family – known in the bible as the sons of God. They are also elohim. His spirit children.

Yahweh is composed of three beings in one - Father, Son, and Holy Spirit. The three are indistinguishable in appearance, in essence, and in purpose, yet distinguishable as individuals when needs be.

Although unified, members of the trinity of Yahweh can act independently.

Yahweh is holy, a perfect elohim, and as such is the source of all authority, all knowledge, morality, light, goodness, love, and truth.

Yahweh is male and created the Earth and all things that exist upon the Earth, above the Earth, in the Earth, beneath the Earth, and around it.

Yahweh as creator holds the power to annihilate anything that he has made.

It is also impossible for darkness to exist around Yahweh because Yahweh radiates light.

It is also impossible for any living soul that is not perfect (sinless) to exist in close proximity to Yahweh, because of his righteous nature and power.

From time-to-time, throughout biblical history Yahweh has appeared as an angel, as Jesus, and as himself, occasionally simultaneously.

There exists in heaven a divine Council led by Yahweh and composed of seventy spirit beings (elohim), selected from the many sons of God.

The purpose and authority of the Heavily Council members varies according to their rank.

Angels are elohim and act as divine messengers of Yahweh, they also have varied status (archangel etc.).

Other beings worshiped by mankind as God are false Gods! Be they named Allah, Buddha, Krishna, or whatever. These so called Gods may be spirit beings (elohim), like the true God, but they are lesser fallen spirits, or non-existent imaginations, or man-made idols – they are not God!

CREATION

(To simplify the narrative hereafter Yahweh will be defined as God).

God decided to create other beings to add to his family.

In order to achieve this desire, God first created Earth.

When God had finished making the Earth God said that it was good. His intention was for it to remain good. Good does not mean perfect.

The completed Earth was dynamic and chaotic, and contained rivers, seas, oceans, mountains, plains, and valleys.

A myriad of benign plant life, and other varied creatures of all types inhabited the whole Earth. These were made for the benefit and enjoyment of man, and for him to manage, and control.

MAN

The first man was created by God in his own likeness or image (to possess the nature and appearance of God). We are meant to be imagers of God - to be like him!

The word 'man' translated, means 'Adam'.

God formed Adam from the dust of the Earth. He breathed life into him, and subsequently, Adam became a living creature, a soul!

EDEN

God provided for all Adam's needs in a mountainous region upon the Earth known as Eden.

The word 'Eden' translated from several ancient languages, means 'heavenly place upon a mountain'. Eden was not the whole Earth. It was a particular place upon the Earth for man to live, and for God to walk with man, and to communicate with him. A facsimile of God's heaven upon Earth!

In Eden God planted a garden with beautiful trees having edible fruit. A river watered the garden. Adam lived in the garden and tended it.

Adam was instructed to name all the living creatures that he encountered.

Adam was a sinless soul and as such could walk and talk with God in the Garden of Eden without fear of destruction.

God taught Adam how to live upon the Earth.

God knew that it was not good for Adam to be alone.

It was God's plan for Adam to produce offspring. To do this God put Adam to sleep and created a woman from the rib of Adam.

Upon Adams awakening God introduced the woman to him. Adam named her Eve, because the name meant that she was part of Adam.

Eve was also sinless and could walk and talk with God.

God introduced Eve to Adam. She was his wife, and he was instructed to hold fast to her as a lifelong companion.

Eve, being part of Adam, and the two being male and female, it was now possible for them to be united as one, and thus to be able to reproduce offspring in sexual harmony.

Under the marriage covenant sexual activity between husband and wife is not a sin.

Adam and Eve, as eternal beings, had no need for clothing, and in the garden they could eat and drink whatsoever they so desired. However, God commanded the two not to eat from a certain tree that grew in the garden, known as the Tree of Knowledge, or they would definitely die.

WAR IN HEAVEN

There was discontent in the Council of Heaven because a once righteous divine being of light (an elohim) known as the Shining one, a cherubim who guarded the throne of God, vainly wanted God's power and authority for himself. He wanted to be

God.

In some ancient languages, the name 'Shining one', can also be translated as 'Serpent', or 'Satan', as in modern biblical translations. Hereafter we shall refer to him by that name, although nowhere in the Hebrew Old Testament is that name used for this evil elohim, but the Hebrew word 'nachesh', a spirit being, is used.

This unrighteous, clever, and rebellious elohim caused a war to break out in heaven, and a number of other elohim inhabiting heaven, having free will, took the side of Satan.

God did not destroy the rebellious spirits', but cast them down to Earth from heaven to reside upon the Earth. Here they became known as evil spirits, fallen angels, or demons.

Evil spirits do not have bodies but have the capacity to appear in dreams and visions, taking any form that they wish, including false Gods.

These demons have free will, and observing all, have existed upon the Earth from its foundation, gaining experience, and having communicable knowledge that they can use to deceive.

In certain circumstances these demons can possess individuals and take control of their faculties (e.g. biblical Legion).

Cast down, Satan knew what God was planning and had access to the Garden of Eden.

RUINATION – A METAPHOR

In the Garden of Eden Satan appeared to Eve as himself (an elohim), and told her a falsehood so that she might wilfully disobey God's commandment and sin.

Satan told Eve that God was a liar, and that if she ate of the forbidden fruit, that she would not die, as God had foretold, but would become wise, and comparable to God.

Subsequently, having free will, Eve did eat, and then gave some of the fruit to Adam, who was standing beside her.

Satan considered that once sin had entered the world through Eve, God's plan for an eternal family would be destroyed, decreasing God's power and authority in heaven and increasing his own.

Having tasted the fruit, Adam and Eve realised that they had sinned and were naked, and becoming frightened, they went and hid from God in the garden.

In hiding, Adam and Eve made coverings for themselves from fig leaves to conceal their nakedness.

Upon discovering Adam and Eve, God asked them how they knew that they were naked, and Eve told him that Satan had tricked her.

THE OUTCOME OF SINNING

Because of what Satan had done, God cursed him above all creatures. It is recorded that God told Satan that he would go on his belly and eat dust forever. That God would put enmity (hatred) between Eve's seed (children) and Satan's seed. That Satan could bruise the heel of mankind, but God gave mankind the power to bruise the head of Satan.

This curse was written down in scripture as a metaphor, signifying that Satan was to remain thrust down upon the Earth without heavenly authority. Here with his spirit followers, he would become the unseen ruler of the Earth, or prince of darkness. Lord of the dead. In charge of Sheol, the grave. The very opposite of what Satan had desired.

God told Eve that because of what she had done, henceforth, giving birth would be painful, and that her desires would not be the same as what Adam desired. However, Adam was to have dominion over her.

As for Adam, because he had followed Eve's direction, God decreed that Adam would no longer get an easy living, but the Earth would become cursed for his sake. He would have to work painfully by the sweat of his brow for the rest of his life, before his body would return to the dust from whence it came.

God made clothing out of animal skins for the couple, and they removed their makeshift leafy coverings of fig leaves and dressed.

AFTERWARDS

In the east of Eden grew another tree known as the Tree of Life. If Adam and Eve had eaten of the fruit of this tree then they would have existed upon Earth forever and never died.

Because there was a risk that Adam and Eve might eat of the Tree of Life and live forever in their sins, and never be able to return to Gods presence, God forced Adam and Eve to leave the Garden of Eden and to go out into the world to fend for themselves.

To the east of the Garden of Eden God placed a special elohim, a cherubim, to guard Eden so that Adam and Eve could not return and access the Tree of Life.

Adam and Eve's task as imagers of God was to organise the chaotic Earth and to populate it by procreating and raising children. This they began to do.

Eventually Adam and Eve grew old, both dying, and their bodies returned to the earth, and becoming elohim, their spirits departed to God's absentee care, not to heaven. Because of their sinning they were unable to come back into God's presence, seemingly forever.

INNOCENCE

Original sin is not transferred to siblings. Adam and Eves guilt and culpability is not passed on to their issue, neither is ours.

Babies begin their life as soon as an egg is fertilised and begins growing in the mother's womb. As the child grows nutrients are drawn from the host mother, but the baby remains an independent separate entity.

As with Eve, a woman's body belongs to herself, and she can decide what to do with it, but what may be maturing in her womb does not belong to her, and is a genetically distinct separate being. She cannot speak or make decisions on its behalf.

Children who have not reached, or obtained the mental maturity to sin consciously - perhaps aborted, miscarried, have otherwise died in infancy, or are incapable of rationalisation, will be resurrected as a perfect soul at the first resurrection, and will not be judged. God is just.

Adam and Eve's issue were born righteous, just as you and I were, but having free will, it was impossible for us to remain innocent and not to sin sooner or later, everyone does. That is why we are all sinners.

It remains impossible for innocent children not to sin, because they have free will. All mankind, whatever age, inherently knows how to do evil naturally, to a greater or lesser extent. As children we have to be taught how to be good, and how to avoid evil.

That is why the Earth is always at war, full of wickedness, famine and pollution, and why it will be ultimately destroyed, and then renewed.

THE PLAN OF SALVATION

The death of Adam and Eve, with their bodies remaining lifeless upon the earth, and their spirits gone elsewhere, brought about their and our separation from God. Even if later on their fallen bodies were to be resurrected, and again united with their spirits, they would exist as sinners for eternity. Unrighteous beings unable to come into the presence of God without being destroyed.

However, God knew what Satan was capable of, and unknown to Satan, made a way for all of mankind to return to his presence cleansed of sin, should they wish to be.

But in order to satisfy justice and not to rob mercy (or God would not be God), there is a just price that must be paid for all of our sinning. The price is one sinless death!

PROBLEM

Because we are all sinners we cannot pay the price for sin for ourselves.

We need someone sinless to pay the price on our behalf. To be the price payer, or the Redeemer! He cannot be just a man, because all mankind sin, so he has to be something else, but what?

THE REDEEMER

When God asked for a volunteer to pay the price for sin (to be the Redeemer), the Son of God, said, "Here I am, send me!"

So God sent his Son (an elohim) to the Earth, to be born of a virgin, as a man. Born of a virgin because the Redeemer was the Son of God, and not the product of the seed of Joseph, the husband of Mary. Jesus became God and Man!

In Hebrew the Son of God was to be named Yeshua, and later to be known as Jesus, in Greek – a name that means 'He who saves'. The name was decided before Jesus came to Earth.

As both man and God, Jesus would ultimately live a sinless life, teach Adam's seed how to live righteously, cast out demons, and as God the Messiah (Saviour) and Redeemer offer his body as a sinless sacrifice for *all* sinners.

After Jesus lay dead in a tomb for three days, and his spirit had been elsewhere, God resurrected his lifeless body and reunited it again with his spirit. The first fruits of them that slept. The first man to be resurrected. A new and perfect being.

Eventually Jesus ascended into heaven and as a king, sinless, sits at God's right hand.

A FACT

The destruction of the Earth is prophesised to take place soon, and Jesus has promised to return at that juncture, bringing redeemed (the just) resurrected beings with him. Then he will create a new heaven and a new Earth, and along with his sinless subjects, he will rule justly from a New Jerusalem, as King of kings for all eternity.

WHAT WILL HAPPEN TO ME?

After your death your body will remain upon the Earth and your spirit will pass into the care of God (not to heaven), as an elohim. There in the spiritual realm, in full remembrance of your past life, you will wait for the resurrection of your lifeless body, and the unification of your spirit. When your resurrection happens, you will become an eternal living soul.

HOW DOES THAT WORK?

After Jesus returns to Earth the second time there

will be two resurrections – The first resurrection will be composed of the just (those who accepted the redemption of Jesus), and then much later, the unjust will be resurrected (those who rejected Jesus). Everyone who ever lived will be resurrected.

The just will become new souls, when their redeemed spirits (renewed from the spirit world), and their lifeless bodies (resurrected from the grave) are reunited in sinless perfection.

The just will live with Jesus (God) upon a new Earth (not in heaven!) as his children, for all eternity. Thus fulfilling the original intention of God in the Garden of Eden by becoming new members of the family of God.

The unredeemed will have to wait until judgement day to learn their fate! Some no doubt in torment.

Upon judgement day the unjust will be judged for every sin that they have ever committed, and receiving differing judgments, they will be sent somewhere else other than the new Earth? Or annihilated!

CONCLUSION

Surprise, if you wish you can chose to disregard pages 1-to here, but do not overlook what follows!

The good news is that Jesus has paid the price for your sins by dying upon a cross!

Should you wish to take advantage of the fact that Jesus has paid for your sinning, and not have to pay the penalty for your own sins (there is no compulsion), then you must invite him into your life, and become born again.

How can you be born again? This is an old biblical question.

TO BE BORN AGAIN

Accept Jesus as your Saviour and Redeemer.

Repent of your sins (stop sinning), and confess as many sins as you can think of to Jesus. Do this vocally, and in secret. Only he can forgive you.

Stopping sinning, is not as hard as you might suppose – God helps you!

Follow the teachings of Jesus until you die.

Try your hardest not to sin again, you will sin again, we all do, to a greater or lesser extent, so keep repenting.

THE OUTCOME

If you have accepted Jesus - HALLELUJAH! You are on the road to salvation – keep on going.

Should you reject Jesus and his free gift of

redemption, then you will remain in your sins forevermore.

Make no mistake - all those who have ever lived will be judged. You and I will be judged, and either, forgiven and redeemed, or else be shut out of God's presence forever, or be annihilated.

Do not be deceived, Satan is real, a place named Hell exists, and is reserved for Satan and his angels (wicked elohim) – and some notable others.

Sinners do not escape without punishment.

Do not end up in Hell. You cannot say that you have not been warned - act now!

ADVICE

Take my advice, repent, and pray in secret, and audibly, to God the Eternal Father, every day.

What matters most to God is doing his will and keeping his commandments, not merely believing in him.

Ask God to keep you from the influence of Satan and his demons. Believe me, they are real enough.

Pray that God will guide you in truth and in righteousness for the rest of your short life.

Obtain an English Standard Version Bible and

study it, not simply read it, be a Berean.

Get to know, to love, to fear, and to obey God, and he will get to know and to love you more than you can ever imagine. He is your heavenly father – your creator, become part of his eternal family.

FINALLY

As a tiddler George soon discovered that cool was not warm, up was not down, bad was not good, and that he possessed free will to act however he chose, even if that choice lead to a detrimental situation.

No-one could validate these facts on his behalf. If he swallowed gravel, he got a tummy ache, if he sucked it, and then spat it out, it did him no harm. So he took care, and with experience, George gained knowledge.

Nowadays, enjoying that peace that passes all understanding, George hopes that some of what he has realised will help you understand existence.

But beware, George recognises that motivated by various twisted ideologies, and base desires, there are many fishy creatures in the fish tank that would have him believe, and act, in such a way that is detrimental and ultimately destructive to his eternal soul.

Additionally George knows that the majority of faith fishes in the fish tank are being led in the wrong direction by the indoctrinated well-meaning, therefore George keeps on learning, and does not permit any fish or fishes to instruct him what to believe.

As conditions in the fish tank increasingly deteriorate, and the water gets cloudier, and wickedness increases, George concedes that some aspects of faith have become more obscure, but one truism remains crystal-clear to George - The Big fish exist...

George asks the Big Fish to forgive him if he has made any errors in publishing what he believes to be the truth, and if he has made doctrinal mistakes, for him to remove the memory of them from your mind...

'The kingdom of heaven is like a net that was let down into the lake and caught all kinds of fish. When it was full the fishermen pulled it up on the shore. Then they sat down and collected the good fish in baskets, but threw the bad away'.

Mathew, Chapter 13: verses 47-48.

Love in Yeshua,
George...

ABOUT THE AUTHOR

Before he became a new fish, Peter led a varied and mostly irreverent life during which he published several secular novels and books of poetry.

These included:

Interplanetary Milkmen.
Fists and Flowers.
Josh's Story.
Peter John Scott's Poems.

They can be purchased online by searching amazon books.

E-mail: writessc@supanet.com

27637572R00057

Printed in Great Britain
by Amazon